The Ultimate C... Recipe Book 2022

Over 100 Proven, Classic & Modern Cocktail Recipes with Easy to Follow Instructions for Every Day. (Gin, Vodka, Whiskey, Rum, Non-Alcoholic and More)

Author: Oliver Jones

Contents

Beginner's Tips For Making Cocktails Easy

Have you ever wanted to start making cocktails, but felt daunted by the whole process? There is a huge amount to learn, but that doesn't mean you can't do it – you just need to get started. You will soon be impressing all of your friends with your incredible cocktail skills.

Being able to make cocktails is an amazing party trick that a lot of people would love to have, and it's one that will get you invited to loads of events and fun nights out. Your friends will love you if you can make incredible, unique, and delicious drinks for them to try.

So, what do you need to know before you start making cocktails?

Get Some Equipment

You can't make cocktails with just alcohol and a few glasses; it won't go well. Instead, you need to make sure you have a few gadgets that will help. You should get:

- A shaker: You have various options when choosing a shaker, but a Boston shaker has both a mixing glass and a shaking tin, making it a very versatile and popular choice.

- A strainer: There are many options here, but a Hawthorne strainer is generally considered the best. It uses a coiled spring that will help to keep ingredients in place.

- A sharp knife: This will be necessary for cutting ingredients, so make sure you have a sharp, suitable blade.

- A mixing spoon: Also known as a barspoon, these tend to have a twisted stem that will better mix liquids. You can use the spoon for measuring and stirring, and it doesn't matter enormously what kind you choose when you are just beginning.

- A measure: You need to be able to measure the amount of alcohol you are using if you want to make reliably good cocktails, otherwise the quantities will change and your drinks will sometimes taste odd.

7

- A hand juicer: Although you don't absolutely have to have a hand juicer, it will make certain kinds of cocktails much quicker and easier to create. If you don't want to buy one, make sure you have access to another kind of juicer.

You may also want to buy a muddler, which is an unvarnished wooden stick that is used to lightly crush berries and herbs to encourage them to release juices and flavour. It isn't a necessary piece of equipment as you can do the same thing with other tools when you are just starting out, but it's worth considering.

Don't Forget The Ice

What's the most crucial ingredient in a cocktail? Ice! You need a good amount of it for every drink you make. If you don't add enough ice to the glass, the ice you do add will melt quickly, and this will cause the drink to get diluted.

You need to have a ready supply of ice whenever you want to make cocktails, so grab a few ice cube trays and stock up in advance. This is cheaper and more environmentally friendly than buying ready-made ice.

Choose Your Alcohol

Selecting the alcohol should be done with care. You may want to focus on a few basic cocktails at first so you don't have to buy an enormous amount of liquor to start with. For a Margarita, you'll need tequila and Cointreau, while for something like a Martini, you'll need a dry vermouth and some gin.

You should be choosing high quality alcohol so you can guarantee that the flavour will be good, but you can generally get away with younger spirits, rather than paying the top price for really expensive ones. This should help to keep your budget reasonably low during the early stages, allowing you to stock up on alcohol gradually.

7 Rules For Making A Delicious Cocktail In An Easy & Quick Way

So, how do you actually make cocktails? Let's find out!

Rule 1) Don't Be Afraid Of The Alcohol

Because cocktails often contain other ingredients, some people tend to skimp on the alcohol and pay attention to things like creamers, juices, mixers, and more. Don't do this. The alcohol is the main part of the drink. It's the whole point.

Your cocktail should be at least 50 ml of whatever spirit you have chosen for the base, and then some further alcohol, depending on what you want to add. If you would rather just stick with your basic alcohol, you can do so, but you should pour generously. The point of cocktails is the alcohol.

Rule 2) Focus On Presentation

If you've ever heard the saying that you take the first bite with your eyes, it's time to convert that to drinks. The first sip should be a visual feast of beauty. Pay attention to what your cocktails look like in the glass.

What colours are you using and how do they complement each other? What blend of drinks have you got? What garnishes are you adding and what does that do to the overall appearance of the cocktail? If you are adding a sprig of green mint, for example, is that going to go with the other hues to make something visually stunning?

It isn't just about the flavour; it's about the beauty of the drink. Take the time to make your cocktails look enticing, and you'll find that this enhances the taste considerably!

Rule 3) Pay Attention To Each Ingredient

What are you adding to your cocktail? Every single thing you put in the glass will alter the flavour, texture, and appearance – so don't include things mindlessly. Think hard about it. Are you choosing lemons or limes? Are you adding mint leaves or a squeeze of citrus? Do you want cherries or raspberries? What flavour rum are you going to opt for?

Neglecting to think about these things might feel freeing, but it's not going to create amazing cocktails. Instead, you need to fully consider what will make your drinks shine. Avoid just tossing things in a glass, and instead take a scientific approach to your cocktails – and they will be a million times better for it.

Rule 4) Experiment

Despite the above tip, you shouldn't be afraid to try things out. You don't always have to follow a recipe and only use the top end ingredients in every drink you make. Let yourself try things. Buy cheaper alcohol options, rather than always choosing top shelf bottles. Try swapping one kind of fruit for another.

Cocktail making should be fun as well as an art. If you aren't having a good time with it, you're doing something wrong, so slow down and relax. You want mixing drinks to be a pleasure, not a source of stress.

You should also not worry if you make a mistake and your cocktail doesn't come out perfectly – just learn for next time. It doesn't have to taste perfect every time you have a go, and you might come up with some amazing twists on the classic recipes this way.

Rule 5) Shake Cocktails That Contain Fruit Juice

Have you ever wondered about that famous "shaken, not stirred" line? It turns out that Bond was doing it wrong – because a Martini doesn't contain fruit juice, and it shouldn't be shaken at all. You only need to shake cocktails that have fruit juice in them, because you want to make sure that the juice thoroughly mixes with the spirits and the ice.

Cocktails that only contain alcohol can simply be stirred; there is no need to shake them. Shaking agitates the liquids and forces them to mix, but spirits should mix simply by stirring them briskly. You can therefore save yourself some time and energy by stirring aromatic cocktails (alcohol-only drinks) and shaking the ones that contain other ingredients.

Rule 6) Focus On Balance

Many of us think of cocktails as drinks that should make you gasp when you first taste them, but there is a lot more to it than that. Your cocktail needs to taste good as well as impressive. You want to make sure that the last drops are as delicious as the first sip – and that means focusing on getting the flavours to balance.

Are you adding lemon to your drink? What's going to balance that out and stop it from being sour? Are you adding something sharp and refreshing like mint? What will make it mellower?

No matter what ingredients you are putting in, make sure you are thinking about the balance and keeping everything in check so that your drinks taste great no matter what.

Rule 7) Stay Simple

Especially as a beginner, this is a very important rule to follow. Don't add thirty kinds of liquor to one cup, or even buy thirty kinds of liquor when you first begin. A cocktail can be delicious in its simplicity. You don't need to go crazy. The best cocktails tend to be the ones that you can create again and again and again, working on them until you have a perfect blend of the ingredients.

Of course, you can splash out and buy a more unusual liquor now and again if you want to, but don't feel that you need to. You can make a wide range of cocktails with just the basics, so you don't need to dedicate an entire section of your kitchen to alcohol and other ingredients. A few simple bottles will do.

You should apply this rule even more firmly to the individual drinks you make. Most cocktails don't have more than three ingredients. There's nothing wrong with branching out and experimenting a bit, but if you add too much to the glass, it'll turn into a mess of flavours, rather than an enjoyable drink. You won't be able to taste everything, so you'll end up with a confusing muddle instead.

Try to avoid this and keep things simple. Use ingredients that you know and feel confident with, and use recipes if you want to branch out.

3 Common Mistakes To Avoid

Now that you know some of the commonest rules to follow, what about things you should avoid doing? There are mistakes you can make even with something as simple as mixing drinks, so let's find out where people tend to go wrong when they first begin making cocktails. Once you know what the commonest mistakes are, you can make sure you avoid them!

Mistake 1) Not Chilling Ingredients

We talked earlier about the necessity of using ice in your cocktails and making sure you have enough ice to ensure that it doesn't melt quickly, but a lot of people don't realise that they should try to chill the other ingredients too if they can. If possible, you should chill your bottles of alcohol, and cool your cocktail glasses with ice or cold water.

Mistake 2) Adding Too Many Mixers

Mixers are a popular part of cocktails, but don't depend on them too much; they can mess up the flavour of your drink. Mixers tend to contain sweeteners and e numbers that you don't necessarily want in your drinks.

Mistake 3) Running Before You Can Walk

It might be tempting to try making some really complex cocktails when you first get going – but it's better to start with the classics and learn how to balance the flavours and different ingredients before you do this.

What Are The 4 Methods Of Making A Cocktail?

So, how do you make a cocktail? Let's find out!

Method 1) Stirring

We mentioned stirring earlier. As the name suggests, this simply involves using a stirrer and then straining the drink into a glass. This is usually used for liqueurs, spirits, etc.

Method 2) Shaking

Cocktails that include fruit juices, syrups, cream, eggs, etc., need to be shaken in a proper shaker in order to make sure they mix properly and taste good.

Method 3) Building

With this method, you pour the ingredients into the glass one at a time, and then stir them lightly to combine them.

Method 4) Blending

For this, you need an electric blender. It is used for making large amounts of mixed drinks. Make sure you puree any fruit before adding ice. This tends to be more time consuming, but it's great if you want to add solids to your drinks.

Alcoholic Cocktail Recipes

Blue Glowtini

Serving|1   Time|10 minutes
Nutritional Content (per serving):
Cal| 178   Fat| 0g   Protein| 0.1g   Carbs| 11.1g   Fiber| 0.1g

Ingredients:

- ❖ 115 millilitres (½ fluid ounces) citrus-infused vodka
- ❖ 15 millilitres (½ fluid ounce) blue curacao
- ❖ 30 millilitres (1 fluid ounce) liquid prepared sweet and sour mix
- ❖ 15 millilitres (½ fluid ounce) peach schnapps
- ❖ 30 millilitres (1 fluid ounce) pineapple juice
- ❖ Ice cubes, as required

Directions:

1. Fill a cocktail shaker with ice.
2. Add remaining ingredients into the shaker.
3. Cover the cocktail shaker with lid and shake vigorously for about 30 seconds.
4. Strain into a serving glass and serve.

Dole Whip Float

Servings|4   Time|10 minutes
Nutritional Content (per serving):
Cal| 296   Fat| 8.6g   Protein| 2g   Carbs| 29.9g   Fiber| 3.1g

Ingredients:

- 690 grams (4 cups) frozen pineapple
- 180 millilitres (6 fluid ounces) rum
- 240 millilitres (1 cup) unsweetened coconut milk
- 1 frozen banana

Directions:

1. In a high-power blender, add all ingredients and pulse until smooth.
2. Serve immediately.

Pisco Sour

Servings|2   Time|10 minutes
Nutritional Content (per serving):
Cal| 151   Fat| 0.6g   Protein| 2.4g   Carbs| 19.6g   Fiber| 2.4g

Ingredients:

- ❖ 60 millilitres (2 fluid ounces) Pisco Quebranta
- ❖ 150 millilitres (5 fluid ounces) lime juice
- ❖ 30 grams (1 ounce) egg white
- ❖ Ice cubes, as required
- ❖ 150 millilitres (5 fluid ounces) lemon juice
- ❖ 30 grams (1 ounce) gum syrup
- ❖ 6 drops Angostura bitters

Directions:

1. In a cocktail shaker, add the Pisco Quebranta, lemon juice, lime juice, gum syrup and angostura bitters.
2. Cover the cocktail shaker with lid and shake vigorously for about 30 seconds.
3. Pour into 2 tall glasses.
4. Fill with ice cubes and serve.

Wine Spritzer

Serving|2   Time|10 minutes
Nutritional Content (per serving):
Cal| 71   Fat| 0g   Protein| 0.1g   Carbs| 2.3g   Fiber| 0g

Ingredients:

- ❖ Ice cubes, as required
- ❖ 180 millilitres (6 fluid ounces) chilled white wine
- ❖ 60 millilitres (2 fluid ounces) cold club soda
- ❖ 2 lime slices

Directions:

1. Fill 2 glasses with ice and top with the wine, followed by the soda.
2. Garnish each glass with a lemon slice and serve.

Passion Fruit Spritzer

Serving|1   Time|10 minutes
Nutritional Content (per serving):
Cal| 120   Fat| 0.4g   Protein| 1.3g   Carbs| 13.3g   Fiber| 5.9g

Ingredients:

- ❖ 30 millilitres (1 fluid ounce) vodka
- ❖ 30 millilitres (1 fluid ounce) club soda
- ❖ 60 millilitres (2 fluid ounces) passion fruit juice
- ❖ Ice cubes, as required

Directions:

1. In a cocktail shaker, add the vodka, fruit juice and club soda.
2. Cover the cocktail shaker with lid and shake vigorously for about 30 seconds.
3. Pour into a Champagne flute glass.
4. Fill with ice cubes and serve.

19

Red Sangria

Servings|6   Time|10 minutes
Nutritional Content (per serving):
Cal| 231   Fat| 0.1g   Protein| 0.7g   Carbs| 25.4g   Fiber| 0.7g

Ingredients:

- ❖ 1 (750-millilitre) (25-fluid ounce) bottle fruity red wine
- ❖ 90 grams (3 ounces) simple syrup
- ❖ Ice cubes, as required
- ❖ 120 millilitres (4 fluid ounces) brandy
- ❖ 165 grams (1 cup) mixed fruit chunks (oranges, lemons and lime), seeded

Directions:

1. In a pitcher, add fruit, brandy, wine and simple syrup and stir to combine.
2. Refrigerate to chill for about 4-8 hours.
3. Fill each wine glass with ice and pour sangria on top.
4. Serve immediately.

Apple Cider Sangria

Servings|6   Time|10 minutes
Nutritional Content (per serving):
Cal| 305   Fat| 0.4g   Protein| 0.8g   Carbs| 37.2g   Fiber| 4.4g

Ingredients:

- 1 (750-millilitre) (25-fluid ounce) bottle dry white wine
- 480 millilitres (2 cups) club soda
- 2 Granny Smith apples, cored and cut into 1-inch square cubes
- 1 orange, sliced and seeded
- 8-10 whole cloves
- 480 millilitres (2 cups) apple cider
- 2 shots cinnamon liquor
- 2 shots apple liquor
- 2 honey crisp apples, cored and cut into 1-inch square cubes
- 4 cinnamon sticks

Directions:

1. In a large-sized pitcher, add all ingredients and stir to combine.
2. Refrigerate for at least 3 hours before serving.

Lime Daiquiri

Servings|2   Time|10 minutes
Nutritional Content (per serving):
Cal| 208   Fat| 0.1g   Protein| 0.1g   Carbs| 6.1g   Fiber| 0.1g

Ingredients:

- ❖ 90 millilitres (3 fluid ounces) light rum
- ❖ 10 grams (2 teaspoons) white sugar
- ❖ 60 millilitres (2 fluid ounces) triple sec
- ❖ Ice cubes, as required
- ❖ 2 lime wedges

Directions:

1. In a high-power blender, add all the ingredients and pulse until smooth.
2. Transfer into serving glasses and serve with the garnishing of lime wedges.

Pineapple & Mango Daiquiri

Servings|2   Time|10 minutes
Nutritional Content (per serving):
Cal| 310   Fat| 0.1g   Protein| 0.2g   Carbs| 18.6g   Fiber| 0.1g

Ingredients:

- ❖ 4 (45-millilitre) (1½-fluid ounce) jiggers mango nectar
- ❖ 2 (45-millilitre) (1½-fluid ounce) jiggers triple sec
- ❖ 30 millilitres (2 tablespoons) fresh lime juice
- ❖ 2 (45-millilitre) (1½-fluid ounce) jiggers pineapple juice
- ❖ 2 (45-millilitre) (1½-fluid ounce) jiggers rum
- ❖ 645 grams (3 cups) ice cubes

Directions:

1. In a high-power blender, add all the ingredients except the ice and pulse until smooth.
2. Add the ice and pulse highest setting until slushy.
3. Transfer into serving glasses and serve.

Banana Daiquiri

Servings|2   Time|10 minutes
Nutritional Content (per serving):
Cal| 220   Fat| 0.2g   Protein| 0.7g   Carbs| 19.8g   Fiber| 1.8g

Ingredients:

- 1 large banana, peeled and sliced
- 60 millilitres (2 fluid ounces) fresh lime juice
- 10 grams (2 teaspoons) white sugar
- 90 millilitres (3 fluid ounces) light rum
- 30 millilitres (1 fluid ounce) triple sec
- Ice cubes, as required

Directions:

1. In a high-power blender, add all the ingredients except the ice and pulse until smooth.
2. Add the ice and pulse highest setting until slushy.
3. Transfer into serving glasses and serve.

24

Beer Margarita

Servings|6   Time|10 minutes
Nutritional Content (per serving):
Cal| 356   Fat| 0g   Protein| 0.8g   Carbs| 42g   Fiber| 0.1g

Ingredients:

- 360 millilitres (12 fluid ounces) cans beer
- 360 millilitres (1½ cups) gold tequila
- 1 lime, cut into 6 wedges
- 1 (340-gram) (12-ounce) can limeade concentrate
- Ice cubes, as required

Directions:

1. In a large-sized pitcher, add the beer, limeade and tequila and stir to combine.
2. Fill tall serving glasses with ice cubes and top with the beer mixture.
3. Squeeze 1 lime wedge into each glass and serve.

Citrus Margarita

Serving|1 Time|10 minutes
Nutritional Content (per serving):
Cal| 175   Fat| 0.1g   Protein| 0.4g   Carbs| 9g   Fiber| 0.7g

Ingredients:

- ❖ 60 millilitres (2 fluid ounces) fresh pink grapefruit juice
- ❖ 60 millilitres (2 fluid ounces) Tequila Blanco
- ❖ 60 millilitres (2 fluid ounces) club soda
- ❖ 15 millilitres (½ fluid ounce) fresh lime juice
- ❖ 30 millilitres (1 fluid ounce) Aperol
- ❖ Ice cubes, as required

Directions:

1. In a cocktail shaker, add the grapefruit juice, lime juice tequila, Aperol and ice.
2. Cover the cocktail shaker with lid and shake vigorously for about 30 seconds.
3. Strain the mixture into an ice-filled glass.
4. Top with club soda and serve.

Strawberry Margarita

Servings|6   Time|10 minutes
Nutritional Content (per serving):
Cal| 260   Fat| 0.2g   Protein| 0.6g   Carbs| 7.6g   Fiber| 2g

Ingredients:

- ❖ 340 grams (12 ounces) frozen limeade concentrate
- ❖ 600 millilitres (20 fluid ounces) tequila
- ❖ 540 millilitres (18 fluid ounces) water
- ❖ 10 fresh strawberries, hulled and sliced
- ❖ 8 fresh basil leaves

Directions:

1. Place limeade concentrate, water, strawberries, basil leaves and tequila and mix well.
2. Cover and refrigerate overnight before serving.

Raspberry Margarita

Serving|1   Time|10 minutes
Nutritional Content (per serving):
Cal| 384   Fat| 0g   Protein| 0.1g   Carbs| 13.8g   Fiber| 0.1g

Ingredients:

- ❖ 60 millilitres (2 fluid ounces) tequila
- ❖ 30 millilitres (1 fluid ounce) fresh lime juice
- ❖ 15 millilitres (½ fluid ounce) raspberry schnapps razzmatazz
- ❖ 30 millilitres (1 fluid ounce) fresh lime juice
- ❖ 15 millilitres (½ fluid ounce) grenadine
- ❖ 30 millilitres (1 fluid ounce) vodka

Directions:

1. Fill a cocktail shaker with ice.
2. Add remaining ingredients into the shaker.
3. Cover the cocktail shaker with lid and shake vigorously for about 30 seconds.
4. Strain into a serving glass and serve.

Mango Margarita

Serving|1 Time|10 minutes
Nutritional Content (per serving):
Cal| 274 Fat| 0.4g Protein| 1.4g Carbs| 32.4g Fiber| 2.4g

Ingredients:

- 60 grams (2 ounces) mango puree
- 30 millilitres (1 fluid ounce) ginger liqueur
- 15 grams (½ ounce) agave syrup
- Ice cubes, as required
- 50 millilitres (1¾ fluid ounces) tequila
- 15 millilitres (½ fluid ounce) fresh lime juice
- 1 Habanero Pepper, sliced finely

Directions:

1. Fill a cocktail shaker with ice.
2. Add remaining ingredients into the shaker.
3. Cover the cocktail shaker with the lid and shake to combine completely.
4. Strain into a serving glass and serve.

Kiwi Margarita

Servings|2   Time|10 minutes
Nutritional Content (per serving):
Cal| 385   Fat| 7.2g   Protein| 1.5g   Carbs| 25g   Fiber| 3g

Ingredients:

- 1120 millilitres (4 fluid ounces) tequila
- ½ lime, peeled and seeded
- 60 millilitres (2 fluid ounces) coconut milk
- Ice cubes, as required
- 60 millilitres (2 fluid ounces) triple sec
- 30 grams (1 ounce) simple syrup
- 2 kiwis, peeled

Directions:

1. In a high-power blender, add all ingredients and pulse until smooth.
2. Serve immediately.

Passion Fruit & Mango Margarita

Serving|1   Time|10 minutes
Nutritional Content (per serving):
Cal| 277   Fat| 0.8g   Protein| 2.7g   Carbs| 38.1g   Fiber| 12.3g

Ingredients:

- ❖ 45 millilitres (1½ fluid ounces) tequila
- ❖ 115 grams (½ cup) passion fruit puree
- ❖ 15 millilitres (½ fluid ounce) fresh lime juice
- ❖ 15 millilitres (½ fluid ounce) ginger liqueur
- ❖ 30 millilitres (1 fluid ounce) mango nectar

Directions:

1. In a high-power blender, add all ingredients and pulse until smooth.
2. Serve immediately.

Avocado Margarita

Serving|1   Time|10 minutes
Nutritional Content (per serving):
Cal| 519   Fat| 19.6g   Protein| 1.9g   Carbs| 31.5g   Fiber| 8.2g

Ingredients:

- ❖ ½ of ripe avocado, peeled and pitted
- ❖ 30 millilitres (1 fluid ounce) melon liqueur
- ❖ Ice cubes, as required
- ❖ 60 millilitres (2 fluid ounces) white 100% agave tequila
- ❖ 30 millilitres (2 tablespoons) fresh lime juice

Directions:

1. In a high-power blender, add all ingredients and pulse until smooth.
2. Serve immediately.

Mint Mojito

Servings|2   Time|15 minutes
Nutritional Content (per serving):
Cal| 129   Fat| 0g   Protein| 0.1g   Carbs| 8.8g   Fiber| 0.2g

Ingredients:

- 20 grams (4 teaspoons) white sugar
- 2 (45-millilitre) (1½-fluid ounce) jiggers lemon-flavored rum
- 6 fresh mint leaves
- 1 lime, cut into 6 wedges
- Ice cubes, as required
- 120 millilitres (½ cup) carbonated water

Directions:

1. In 2 serving glass tumblers, divide the sugar and mint leaves and with the back of a spoon, crush vigorously to release extracts.
2. Add 3 lime wedges into each glass and stir vigorously to release some lime juice.
3. Now, divide the rum into glasses and then fill each with ice cubes.
4. Pour the carbonated water on top and stir well.
5. Serve immediately.

Cucumber Mojito

Serving|1   Time|10 minutes
Nutritional Content (per serving):
Cal| 141   Fat| 0.1g   Protein| 0.5g   Carbs| 2.6g   Fiber| 1.2g

Ingredients:

- 1 lime, quartered
- 10 grams (1 tablespoon) powdered Erythritol
- 60 millilitres (2 fluid ounces) white rum
- 10 fresh mint leaves
- 2 English cucumber slices
- Ice cubes, as required
- 120 millilitres (4 fluid ounces) club soda

Directions:

1. In a highball glass, squeeze the lime quarters.
2. Place the lime quarters, mint leaves and Erythritol in glass and with the back of a spoon, muddle well.
3. Now, place the cucumber slices into the glass and fill with ice cubes.
4. Add the rum and then top with club soda.
5. With a spoon, gently stir and serve.

Cranberry Mojito

Servings|3   Time|10 minutes
Nutritional Content (per serving):
Cal| 174   Fat| 0.1g   Protein| 0.4g   Carbs| 9.4g   Fiber| 2.1g

Ingredients:

- 240 millilitres (1 cup) cranberry juice
- 180 millilitres (6 fluid ounces) light rum
- 10 grams (2 teaspoons) honey
- Ice cubes, as required
- 240 millilitres (1 cup) seltzer water
- 60 millilitres (¼ cup) lime juice
- 10 grams (1/3 cup) fresh mint leaves

Directions:

1. In a pitcher, add cranberry juice, seltzer water, rum, lime juice, mint leaves and honey and stir to combine.
2. Fill 3 glasses with ice and top with cranberry mixture.

White Cosmopolitan

Serving|1   Time|10 minutes
Nutritional Content (per serving):
Cal| 150   Fat| 0g   Protein| 0g   Carbs| 1.8g   Fiber| 0.5g

Ingredients:

- ❖ Ice cubes, as required
- ❖ 30 millilitres (1 fluid ounce) white cranberry juice
- ❖ 15 millilitres (1 tablespoon) fresh lime juice
- ❖ 45 millilitres (1½ fluid ounces) vodka
- ❖ 15 millilitres (½ fluid ounce) triple sec
- ❖ 1 lime slice

Directions:

1. Fill a cocktail shaker with the ice and place the remaining ingredients except the lime slice.
2. Cover the cocktail shaker with lid and shake vigorously for about 30 seconds.
3. Through a strainer, strain into a chilled cocktail glass.
4. Serve with the garnishing of lime slice.

Watermelon Cosmopolitan

Serving|1 Time|10 minutes
Nutritional Content (per serving):
Cal| 284   Fat| 0.4g   Protein| 1.8g   Carbs| 22.8g   Fiber| 1.8g

Ingredients:

- 300 grams (2 cups) watermelon, peeled, seeded and cubed
- 1 mint sprig
- Ice cubes, as required
- 1 (45-millilitres) (1½-fluid ounce) jigger vodka

Directions:

1. In a high-power blender, add the watermelon and pulse until smooth.
2. Through a fine mesh strainer, strain the pureed watermelon into a bowl, discarding the pulp.
3. Fill a cocktail shaker with the ice and place the vodka and watermelon juice.
4. Cover the cocktail shaker with lid and shake vigorously for about 30 seconds.
5. Through a strainer, strain into a chilled cocktail glass.
6. Serve with the garnishing of mint sprig.

Cranberry Cosmopolitan

Serving|1   Time|10 minutes
Nutritional Content (per serving):
Cal| 198   Fat| 0g   Protein| 0g   Carbs| 1.4g   Fiber| 0.5g

Ingredients:

- ❖ Ice cubes, as required
- ❖ 30 millilitres (1 fluid ounce) orange-flavored liqueur
- ❖ 10 millilitres (2 teaspoons) fresh lime juice
- ❖ 60 millilitres (2 fluid ounces) vodka
- ❖ 30 millilitres (1 fluid ounce) cranberry juice

Directions:

1. Fill a cocktail shaker with the ice and place the vodka, liqueur, cranberry juice and lime juice.
2. Cover the cocktail shaker with lid and shake vigorously for about 30 seconds.
3. Through a strainer, strain into a chilled cocktail glass.
4. Garnish with cranberries and serve.

Gin Martini Cocktail

Serving|1   Time|10 minutes
Nutritional Content (per serving):
Cal| 217   Fat| 1.4g   Protein| 0.1g   Carbs| 1.3g   Fiber| 0.4g

Ingredients:

- Ice cubes, as required
- 15 millilitres (½ fluid ounce) dry vermouth
- 75 millilitres (2½ fluid ounces) gin
- 3 olives

Directions:

1. In a martini shaker, add the ice cubes, gin and vermouth.
2. Cover the cocktail shaker with lid and shake vigorously for about 30 seconds.
3. Through a strainer, strain into a chilled cocktail glass.
4. Garnish with olives and serve.

Cranberry Apple Martini

Serving|1   Time|10 minutes
Nutritional Content (per serving):
Cal| 165   Fat| 0g   Protein| 0g   Carbs| 5.2g   Fiber| 2.1g

Ingredients:

- 40 millilitres (1¼ fluid ounces) apple-flavored whiskey
- Ice cubes, as required
- 25 millilitres (¾ fluid ounce) apple schnapps
- 60 millilitres (2 fluid ounces) cranberry juice

Directions:

1. Fill a cocktail shaker with ice.
2. Add remaining ingredients into the shaker.
3. Cover the cocktail shaker with lid and shake vigorously for about 30 seconds.

Orange Martini Cocktail

Serving|1   Time|10 minutes
Nutritional Content (per serving):
Cal| 229   Fat| 0.1g   Protein| 0.2g   Carbs| 25.7g   Fiber| 0.1g

Ingredients:

- Ice cubes, as required
- 30 millilitres (1 fluid ounce) dark rum
- 30 millilitres (1 fluid ounce) orange juice
- 1 thin orange slice
- 30 millilitres (1 fluid ounce) light rum
- 30 millilitres (1 fluid ounce) grenadine
- 5 millilitres (1 teaspoon) fresh lemon juice

Directions:

1. Fill a martini shaker with ice about half way full and place the remaining ingredients.
2. Cover the cocktail shaker with lid and shake vigorously for about 30 seconds.
3. Through a strainer, strain into a chilled cocktail glass.
4. Garnish with orange slice and serve.

Chocolate Martini Cocktail

Serving|1   Time|10 minutes
Nutritional Content (per serving):
Cal| 300   Fat| 7.4g   Protein| 1g   Carbs| 21.5g   Fiber| 1.1g

Ingredients:

- 5 grams (1 teaspoon) chocolate syrup
- 30 millilitres (1 fluid ounce) vanilla vodka
- 30 millilitres (1 fluid ounce) Frangelico
- 30 millilitres (1 fluid ounce) chocolate liqueur
- 30 millilitres (1 fluid ounce) dark crème de cacao
- Ice cubes, as required

Directions:

1. In a martini glass, place the chocolate and swirl around to decorate the glass.
2. In a cocktail shaker, place remaining ingredients.
3. Cover the cocktail shaker with lid and shake vigorously for about 30 seconds.
4. Pour into decorated glass and serve.

Eggnog Cocktail

Serving|12   Time|15 minutes
Nutritional Content (per serving):
Cal| 674   Fat| 34.1g   Protein| 7.3g   Carbs| 54.4g   Fiber| 0.5g

Ingredients:

- 12 eggs (whites and yolks separated)
- 240 millilitres (1 cup) peach brandy
- 480 millilitres (2 cups) peach-flavored bourbon liqueur
- 1 (16-ounc) package confectioners' sugar
- 240 millilitres (1 cup) dark rum
- 1920 grams (8 cups) heavy whipping cream
- Ground nutmeg, for sprinkling

Directions:

1. In a large-sized bowl, add the egg yolks and beat until thickened and light in color.
2. Slowly add the confectioners' sugar and beat until smooth.
3. Slowly add the brandy and rum into egg yolk mixture, stirring continuously until well combined.
4. Cover the bowl and set aside for about 1 hour.
5. In the bowl of egg yolk mixture, add the cream and bourbon and beat until well combined.
6. Refrigerate, covered for about 3-5 hours.
7. In a clean glass bowl, add the egg whites and beat until stiff peaks form.
8. Gently fold the whipped egg whites into the egg yolk mixture.
9. Serve with the sprinkling of nutmeg.

Dragon Cocktail

Serving|1   Time|10 minutes
Nutritional Content (per serving):
Cal| 171   Fat| 0.7g   Protein| 2.4g   Carbs| 14.56g   Fiber| 0.3g

Ingredients:

- 30 millilitres (1 fluid ounce) melon liqueur
- 15 millilitres (½ fluid ounce) green crème de menthe
- 60 millilitres (¼ cup) fresh pineapple juice
- 15 millilitres (½ fluid ounce) peach schnapps
- 60 millilitres (¼ cup) fresh orange juice

Directions:

1. In a container, place all ingredients and stir to combine.
2. In a serving glass, pour over ice and serve immediately.

Mai-Tie Cocktail

Serving|1   Time|10 minutes
Nutritional Content (per serving):
Cal| 256   Fat| 0g   Protein| 0.1g   Carbs| 25.5g   Fiber| 0.8g

Ingredients:

- 30 millilitres (1 fluid ounce) fresh lime juice
- 30 millilitres (1 fluid ounce) light rum
- 15 grams (½ ounce) agave syrup
- Ice cubes, as required
- 30 millilitres (1 fluid ounce) dark rum
- 15 millilitres (½ fluid ounce) orange curacao
- 15 grams (½ ounce) orgeat almond syrup

Directions:

1. Fill a cocktail shaker with ice.
2. Add remaining ingredients into the shaker.
3. Cover the cocktail shaker with lid and shake vigorously for about 30 seconds.
4. Strain into a serving glass and serve.

Manhattan Cocktail

Serving|1   Time|10 minutes
Nutritional Content (per serving):
Cal| 127   Fat| 0g   Protein| 0g   Carbs| 1.5g   Fiber| 0g

Ingredients:

- ❖ Ice cubes, as required
- ❖ 15 millilitres (½ fluid ounce sweet vermouth
- ❖ 1 maraschino cherry
- ❖ 45 millilitres (1½ fluid ounces) bourbon whiskey
- ❖ 1 dash bitters

Directions:

1. Fill a martini shaker with ice and place the whiskey, vermouth and bitters.
2. Cover the cocktail shaker with lid and shake vigorously for about 30 seconds.
3. Transfer into 2 chilled cocktail glasses and garnish each with a cherry.
4. Serve immediately.

Elsa Cocktail

Serving|1   Time|10 minutes
Nutritional Content (per serving):
Cal| 202   Fat| 0g   Protein| 0.1g   Carbs| 16.4g   Fiber| 0g

Ingredients:

- ❖ 90 millilitres (3 fluid ounces) lemonade
- ❖ 15 millilitres (½ fluid ounce) gin
- ❖ 15 millilitres (½ fluid ounce) rum
- ❖ 15 millilitres (½ fluid ounce) tequila
- ❖ 30 millilitres (1 fluid ounce) Sprite
- ❖ 15 millilitres (½ fluid ounce) vodka
- ❖ 15 millilitres (½ fluid ounce) blue curacao
- ❖ Ice cubes, as required

Directions:

1. In a container, place all ingredients and stir to combine.
2. In a serving glass, pour over ice and serve immediately.

Blue Christmas Cocktail

Serving|1   Time|10 minutes
Nutritional Content (per serving):
Cal| 409   Fat| 0g   Protein| 0g   Carbs| 93.5g   Fiber| 0g

Ingredients:

- ❖ 45 millilitres (1½ fluid ounces) Blue Curacao
- ❖ 60 millilitres (2 fluid ounces) coconut lime soda
- ❖ Ice cubes, as required
- ❖ 75 millilitres (2½ fluid ounces) Limonata San Pellegrino

Directions:

1. In the bottom of a serving glass, add blue Curacao and top with some ice.
2. Fill a cocktail shaker with ice.
3. Add remaining ingredients into the shaker.
4. Cover the cocktail shaker with lid and shake vigorously for about 30 seconds.
5. Strain into the serving glass over ice and blue Curacao.
6. Serve immediately.

Long Iceland Cocktail

Serving|1   Time|10 minutes
Nutritional Content (per serving):
Cal| 344   Fat| 0.2g   Protein| 0.2g   Carbs| 18.3g   Fiber| 0.1g

Ingredients:

- 25 millilitres (¾ fluid ounce) triple sec
- 25 millilitres (¾ fluid ounce) white rum
- 25 millilitres (¾ fluid ounce) gin
- 25 millilitres (¾ fluid ounce) fresh lemon juice
- 25 millilitres (¾ fluid ounce) silver tequila
- 25 millilitres (¾ fluid ounce) vodka
- 30 grams (1 ounce) simple syrup
- Cola, as required
- 1 lemon wedge

Directions:

1. Fill a Collins glass with ice.
2. Then add triple sec, tequila, rum, vodka, gin, simple syrup and lemon juice.
3. Top with a splash of cola and gently stir to combine.
4. Garnish with lemon wedge and serve.

Punch Cocktail

Serving|1   Time|10 minutes
Nutritional Content (per serving):
Cal| 226   Fat| 0g   Protein| 25.3g   Carbs| 90.6g   Fiber| 0g

Ingredients:

- 30 millilitres (1 fluid ounce) dark rum
- 90 millilitres (3 fluid ounces) Gorilla Grog
- 10 millilitres (¼ fluid ounce) grenadine
- 30 millilitres (1 fluid ounce) spiced rum
- 15 grams (½ ounce) almond syrup

Directions:

1. Fill a cocktail shaker with ice.
2. Add remaining ingredients into the shaker.
3. Cover the cocktail shaker with lid and shake vigorously for about 30 seconds.
4. Strain into a serving glass and serve.

Fruity Rum Cocktail

Serving|1 Time|10 minutes
Nutritional Content (per serving):
Cal| 224   Fat| 0g   Protein| 0.1g   Carbs| 33.1g   Fiber| 0.1g

Ingredients:

- 45 millilitres (1½ fluid ounce) spiced rum
- 15 millilitres (½ fluid ounce) fresh lime juice
- A few dashes of Angostura Bitters
- 30 grams (1 ounce) passion fruit syrup
- 15 millilitres (½ fluid ounce) pineapple rum
- Ice cubes, as required

Directions:

1. Fill a cocktail shaker with ice.
2. Add remaining ingredients into the shaker.
3. Cover the cocktail shaker with lid and shake vigorously for about 30 seconds.
4. Strain into a serving glass and serve.

Pineapple & Orange Cocktail

Serving|1   Time|10 minutes
Nutritional Content (per serving):
Cal| 310   Fat| 0.2g   Protein| 0.9g   Carbs| 44.4g   Fiber| 0.3g

Ingredients:

- ❖ 60 millilitres (2 fluid ounces) Myers rum
- ❖ 90 millilitres (3 fluid ounces) pineapple juice
- ❖ 1ce cubes, as required
- ❖ 60 millilitres (2 fluid ounces) orange juice
- ❖ 30 millilitres (1 fluid ounce) sour mix

Directions:

1. Fill a cocktail shaker with ice.
2. Add remaining ingredients into the shaker.
3. Cover the cocktail shaker with lid and shake vigorously for about 30 seconds.
4. Strain into a serving glass and serve.

Kombucha Cocktail

Serving|1 Time|10 minutes
Nutritional Content (per serving):
Cal| 263   Fat| 0.3g   Protein| 0.4g   Carbs| 8.1g   Fiber| 0.1g

Ingredients:

- ❖ 60 millilitres (2 fluid ounces) whiskey
- ❖ 5 grams (1 teaspoon) honey
- ❖ Ice cubes, as required
- ❖ 120 millilitres (4 fluid ounces) Kombucha
- ❖ 30 millilitres (1 fluid ounce) lemon juice

Directions:

1. In a cocktail shaker, add the whiskey, Kombucha, honey and lemon juice.
2. Cover the cocktail shaker with lid and shake vigorously for about 30 seconds.
3. Pour into a Collins glass.
4. Fill with ice cubes and serve.

Amaretto & Raspberry Cocktail

Serving|1   Time|10 minutes
Nutritional Content (per serving):
Cal| 213   Fat| 0.4g   Protein| 0.9g   Carbs| 14.5g   Fiber| 0.9g

Ingredients:

- 60 millilitres (2 fluid ounces) vodka
- 5 grams (¼ ounce) simple syrup
- 30 millilitres (1 fluid ounce) club soda
- Ice cubes, as required
- 10 millilitres (¼ fluid ounce) amaretto
- 30 millilitres (1 fluid ounce) orange juice
- 60 grams (2 ounces) raspberries puree

Directions:

1. In a cocktail shaker, add the vodka, amaretto, syrup, orange juice, soda and raspberries puree.
2. Cover the cocktail shaker with lid and shake vigorously for about 30 seconds.
3. Pour into a Collins glass.
4. Fill with ice cubes and serve.

Cucumber Cocktail

Serving|1   Time|10 minutes
Nutritional Content (per serving):
Cal| 237   Fat| 0.1g   Protein| 0.5g   Carbs| 28.2g   Fiber| 0.4g

Ingredients:

- ❖ 60 millilitres (2 fluid ounces) cucumber vodka
- ❖ 60 millilitres (2 fluid ounces) cucumber juice
- ❖ 30 grams (1 ounce) simple syrup
- ❖ 60 millilitres (2 fluid ounces) tonic water
- ❖ 30 millilitres (1 fluid ounce) fresh lime juice
- ❖ Ice cubes, as required
- ❖ 2 fresh mint leaves

Directions:

1. In a cocktail shaker, add the vodka, tonic water, cucumber juice, lime juice and simple syrup.
2. Cover the cocktail shaker with lid and shake vigorously for about 30 seconds.
3. Pour into a tall glass and fill with ice cubes.
4. Garnish with mint leaves and serve.

Fennel Cocktail

Servings|1   Time|10 minutes
Nutritional Content (per serving):
Cal| 248   Fat| 0.2g   Protein| 0.3g   Carbs| 2.9g   Fiber| 0.1g

Ingredients:

- 150 millilitres (5 fluid ounces) don julio blanco
- 5 grams (½ teaspoon) raw honey
- Dash of orange bitters
- Ice cubes, as required
- 1 fennel frond
- 60 millilitres (2 fluid ounces) Figli Finocchietto
- 60 millilitres (2 fluid ounces) lemon juice
- 30 millilitres (1 fluid ounce) sparkling wine

Directions:

1. In a cocktail shaker, add the don julio blanco, Figli Finocchietto, honey, lemon juice, orange bitters and sparkling wine.
2. Cover the cocktail shaker with lid and shake vigorously for about 30 seconds.
3. Pour into a flute glass and fill with ice cubes.
4. Garnish with fennel frond and serve.

Whiskey Cocktail

Servings|2   Time|10 minutes
Nutritional Content (per serving):
Cal| 155   Fat| 0g   Protein| 0g   Carbs| 12.6g   Fiber| 0g

Ingredients:

- ❖ 20 grams (4 teaspoons) simple syrup
- ❖ 4 dashes bitters
- ❖ 2 (45-millilitre) (1½-fluid ounce) jiggers bourbon whiskey
- ❖ 10 millilitres (2 teaspoons) water
- ❖ Ice cubes, as required
- ❖ 2 orange slices
- ❖ 2 maraschino cherries

Directions:

1. In 2 whiskey glasses, divide the syrup, water and bitters and stir to combine.
2. Fill each glass with ice cubes.
3. Pour the bourbon on top.
4. Serve with the garnishing of the orange slices and maraschino cherries.

Espresso Cocktail

Servings|2   Time|10 minutes
Nutritional Content (per serving):
Cal| 95   Fat| 0g   Protein| 0.1g   Carbs| 6g   Fiber| 0g

Ingredients:

- ❖ Ice cubes, as required
- ❖ 60 millilitres (2 fluid ounces) rye whiskey
- ❖ 15 grams (½ ounce) simple syrup
- ❖ 2 dashes of bitters
- ❖ 1120 millilitres (4 fluid ounces) espresso, room temperature
- ❖ 2 (2½-centimete) (1-inch) piece lemon peel

Directions:

1. Fill a cocktail shaker with ice and place the espresso, bourbon, simple syrup.
2. Cover the cocktail shaker with lid and shake vigorously for about 30 seconds.
3. Through a strainer, strain into ice filled glasses.
4. Twist 1 lemon peel over each cocktail and serve.

Lemon Cocktail

Serving|1   Time|10 minutes
Nutritional Content (per serving):
Cal| 133   Fat| 0.1g   Protein| 0.1g   Carbs| 6.4g   Fiber| 0.1g

Ingredients:

- ❖ 5 grams (1 teaspoon) honey
- ❖ Ice cubes, as required
- ❖ 30 millilitres (1 fluid ounce) Irish whiskey
- ❖ 15 millilitres (½ fluid ounce) fresh lemon juice
- ❖ 1 lemon twist

- ❖ 5 grams (1 teaspoon) warm water
- ❖ 10 millilitres (¼ fluid ounce) yellow chartreuse
- ❖ 30 millilitres (1 fluid ounce) chilled champagne

Directions:

1. In a small cup, add the honey and warm water and mix well.
2. Fill a cocktail shaker with ice and place the honey mixture, whiskey, chartreuse and lemon juice.
3. Cover the cocktail shaker with lid and shake vigorously for about 30 seconds.
4. Through a strainer, strain into a chilled flute.
5. Add the champagne and stir to combine.
6. Garnish with lemon twist and serve.

Cranberry & Orange Cocktail

Serving|10   Time|10 minutes
Nutritional Content (per serving):
Cal| 130   Fat| 2.6g   Protein| 1.3g   Carbs| 20.1g   Fiber| 2.8g

Ingredients:

- ❖ 720 millilitres (3 cups) chilled cranberry juice
- ❖ 60 millilitres (¼ cup) orange liqueur
- ❖ ½ orange, cut into slices

- ❖ 720 millilitres (3 cups) chilled champagne
- ❖ 200 grams (2 cups) frozen cranberries

Directions:

1. In a punch bowl, add the cranberry juice, champagne and orange liqueur and stir to combine.
2. Add the cranberries and orange slices and serve immediately.

Blue Cocktail

Serving|1   Time|10 minutes
Nutritional Content (per serving):
Cal| 198   Fat| 0g   Protein| 0g   Carbs| 7.7g   Fiber| 0g

Ingredients:

- ❖ 25 millilitres (¾ fluid ounce) Blue Curacao
- ❖ 180 millilitres (6 fluid ounces) champagne
- ❖ 25 millilitres (¾ fluid ounce) lemon rum

Directions:

1. In a champagne flute, place the blue curacao and lemon rum.
2. Top with the champagne and serve.

Beer & Vodka Cocktail

Serving|10   Time|10 minutes
Nutritional Content (per serving):
Cal| 155   Fat| 0.1g   Protein| 0.3g   Carbs| 17.2g   Fiber| 0.1g

Ingredients:

- ❖ 4 (360-millilitres) (12-fluid ounces) cans light beer
- ❖ 360 millilitres (12 fluid ounces) vodka
- ❖ 2 (340-gram) (12-ounce) cans frozen lemonade concentrate

Directions:

1. In a pitcher, add the beer and lemonade and stir to combine.
2. Add the vodka and stir to combine.
3. Serve immediately.

Bloody Mary Cocktail

Serving|1   Time|10 minutes
Nutritional Content (per serving):
Cal| 211   Fat| 1.4g   Protein| 1.8g   Carbs| 11.5g   Fiber| 1.4g

Ingredients:

- Ice cubes, as required
- 60 millilitres (2 fluid ounces) dry gin
- 10 millilitres (2 teaspoons) Worcestershire sauce
- 1¼ grams (¼ teaspoon) prepared horseradish
- Pinch of garlic powder
- Pinch of ground cumin
- 1¼ grams (¼ teaspoon) ground black pepper
- 1 lime wedge
- 1 (180-millilitre) (6-fluid ounce) can tomato juice
- 30 millilitres (2 tablespoons) fresh lemon juice
- 10 grams (2 teaspoons) hot pepper sauce
- 1¼ grams (¼ teaspoon) celery salt
- Pinch of hot chili powder
- 2 stuffed green olives
- 1 fresh cilantro sprig

Directions:

1. In a cocktail shaker, place the ice, tomato juice, gin, lemon juice, Worcestershire sauce, hot sauce, horseradish and spices.
2. Cover the cocktail shaker with lid and shake vigorously for about 30 seconds.
3. Through a strainer, strain into a highball glass.
4. Garnish with olives, cilantro sprig and lemon wedge and serve.

Watermelon Cocktail

Servings|8   Time|10 minutes
Nutritional Content (per serving):
Cal| 118   Fat| 0.3g   Protein| 1.2g   Carbs| 13g   Fiber| 1.1g

Ingredients:

- 1200 grams (8 cups) chilled watermelon
- 60 millilitres (¼ cup) fresh lime juice
- Ice cubes, as required
- 345 millilitres (1(1½ fluid ounces) coconut water
- 240 millilitres (1 cup) citrus-flavored vodka
- Lime wedges, for garnishing

Directions:

1. In a high-power blender, add the watermelon, coconut water and lime juice and pulse until smooth.
2. Transfer the mixture into a large-sized pitcher with vodka and stir to combine.
3. Pour the mixture into ice-filled glasses and serve with the garnishing of lime wedges.

Blue Iced Tea Cocktail

Serving|1 Time|10 minutes
Nutritional Content (per serving):
Cal| 157 Fat| 0g Protein| 0g Carbs| 4.5g Fiber| 0g

Ingredients:

- 15 millilitres (½ fluid ounce) vodka
- 15 millilitres (½ fluid ounce) rum
- 15 millilitres (½ fluid ounce) Blue Curacao
- 15 millilitres (½ fluid ounce) tequila
- 15 millilitres (½ fluid ounce) gin
- Ice cubes, as required

Directions:

1. Fill a cocktail shaker with ice.
2. Add remaining ingredients into the shaker.
3. Cover the cocktail shaker with lid and shake vigorously for about 30 seconds.
4. Serve immediately.

Peach Iced Tea Cocktail

Serving|1   Time|10 minutes
Nutritional Content (per serving):
Cal| 436   Fat| 0g   Protein| 0g   Carbs| 22.9g   Fiber| 0g

Ingredients:

- Ice cubes, as required
- 30 millilitres (1 fluid ounce) vodka
- 30 millilitres (1 fluid ounce) gold tequila
- 90 millilitres (3 fluid ounces) sweet and sour mix
- 30 millilitres (1 fluid ounce) peach schnapps
- 30 millilitres (1 fluid ounce) gin
- 30 millilitres (1 fluid ounce) rum
- 30 millilitres (1 fluid ounce) cola

Directions:

1. Fill a tall glass with ice cubes.
2. Pour peach schnapps, vodka, gin, tequila and mix.
3. Add sweet and sour mix and stir to combine.
4. Top with cola and serve.

Cherry Beer

Servings|2   Time|5 minutes
Nutritional Content (per serving):
Cal| 221   Fat| 0g   Protein| 3.1g   Carbs| 29.3g   Fiber| 0g

Ingredients:

- ❖ 360 millilitres (1½ cups) cherry juice
- ❖ 2 (360-millilitres) (12-fluid ounce) cans wheat beer

Directions:

1. Divide cherry juice into 2 glasses and top with the beer.
2. Serve immediately.

Vodka Slushie

Serving|1   Time|10 minutes
Nutritional Content (per serving):
Cal| 251   Fat| 0g   Protein| 0g   Carbs| 29.8g   Fiber| 0g

Ingredients:

- ❖ 60 millilitres (2 fluid ounces) citrus vodka
- ❖ 30 grams (1 ounce) simple syrup
- ❖ 60 millilitres (2 fluid ounces) sweet and sour mix
- ❖ Ice cubes, as required

Directions:

1. In a high-power blender, add all ingredients and pulse until smooth.
2. Serve immediately.

68

Watermelon Vodka Slushy

Servings|4   Time|10 minutes
Nutritional Content (per serving):
Cal| 179   Fat| 0g   Protein| 0.1g   Carbs| 13.5g   Fiber| 0g

Ingredients:

- 40 grams (¼ cup) sour patch watermelons
- 240 millilitres (1 cup) lemonade
- 240 millilitres (1 cup) vodka
- 240 millilitres (1 cup) sprite
- Ice cubes, as required

Directions:

1. In a glass bowl, soak the watermelon into vodka overnight.
2. In a high-power blender, add 60 millilitres (2 fluid ounces) flavored vodka, Sprite, lemonade and ice and pulse until well combined.
3. Serve immediately.

Hot Alcoholic Cocktail Recipes

Bourbon Eggnog

Servings|2   Time|20 minutes
Nutritional Content (per serving):
Cal| 544   Fat| 23.8g   Protein| 14.1g   Carbs| 37.9g   Fiber| 0.2g

Ingredients:

- ❖ 2 eggs (whites and yolks separated)
- ❖ 480 millilitres (2 cups) whole milk
- ❖ 2½ millilitres (½ teaspoon) pure vanilla extract
- ❖ 120 millilitres (½ cup) bourbon
- ❖ 50 grams (¼ cup) white sugar
- ❖ 120 grams (½ cup) heavy cream
- ❖ 5 grams (1 teaspoon) nutmeg, grated freshly
- ❖ Pinch of salt

Directions:

1. Add egg yolks in a bowl and with an electric mixer, beat on medium speed until light and smooth.
2. Add in (2 tablespoons) of sugar and mix until well blended. Set aside.
3. In a separate bowl, add egg whites and remaining (2 tablespoons) of sugar and with an electric mixer, beat until peaks form. Set aside.
4. In a small-sized saucepan, combine milk, cream, vanilla, nutmeg, and salt over medium-low heat and cook until small bubbles start to appear, stirring continuously.
5. Remove the pan of milk mixture from heat.
6. Slowly pour warm milk mixture into beaten egg yolks and stir until well blended.
7. Add brandy and stir to combine.
8. Fold in whipped egg white mixture and serve.

Wine Hot Chocolate

Servings|4 Time|25 minutes
Nutritional Content (per serving):
Cal| 436   Fat| 21g   Protein| 9.8g   Carbs| 37.5g   Fiber| 1,8g

Ingredients:

- 720 millilitres (3 cups) whole milk
- 15 grams (1 tablespoon) dark cocoa powder
- Pinch of salt
- 60 grams (4 tablespoons) whipped cream
- 160 grams (1 cup) chocolate chips
- 1 cinnamon stick
- 360 millilitres (1½ cups) red wine
- pinch of salt

Directions:

1. In a large-sized pot, add milk, chocolate chips, cocoa powder, salt, and cinnamon stick over medium heat and cook for about 3-5 minutes or until chocolate chips are dissolved completely, stirring continuously.
2. Stir in the wine and immediately adjust the heat to low.
3. Simmer for about 10 minutes, stirring after every 1 minute.
4. Remove the pot of hot chocolate from heat and discard the cinnamon stick.
5. Transfer the hot chocolate into serving mugs.
6. Top with whipped cream and serve.

Kahlua Hot Chocolate

Servings|2   Time|15 minutes
Nutritional Content (per serving):
Cal| 397   Fat| 17.1g   Protein| 10.7g   Carbs| 49.2g   Fiber| 3.7g

Ingredients:

- 480 millilitres (2 cups) 2% milk, divided
- 40 grams (¼ cup) semisweet chocolate chips
- 1¼ millilitres (¼ teaspoon) vanilla extract
- 30 grams (2 tablespoons) whipped cream
- 45 grams (3 tablespoons) cocoa powder
- 25 grams (2 tablespoons) white sugar
- Pinch of ground cinnamon
- 45 millilitres (3 tablespoons) Kahlua

Directions:

1. In a saucepan, add 60 millilitres (¼ cup) of the milk and cocoa powder and whisk well blended.
2. Place the pan of milk mixture over medium heat and whisk in the remaining milk until smooth.
3. Add in the remaining ingredients except for whipped cream and cook for about 2-3 minutes or until the chocolate is melted, stirring continuously.
4. Remove the pan of milk mixture from heat and stir in the Kahlua.
5. Serve immediately with the topping of whipped cream.

Spiked Latte

Serving|1   Time|10 minutes
Nutritional Content (per serving):
Cal| 319   Fat| 6.7g   Protein| 0.4g   Carbs| 21.3g   Fiber| 0g

Ingredients:

- ❖ 120 millilitres (½ cup) freshly brewed coffee
- ❖ 60 millilitres (¼ cup) Kahlua
- ❖ 15 grams (1 tablespoon) whipped cream
- ❖ 60 millilitres (¼ cup) whole milk
- ❖ 15 millilitres (1 tablespoon)s vodka

Directions:

1. In a small-sized saucepan, add in all ingredients except for whipped cream over medium heat and cook until heated, stirring frequently.
2. Pour the latte into a serving mug and serve immediately with the topping of whipped cream.

Spiked Pumpkin Latte

Serving|1   Time|15 minutes
Nutritional Content (per serving):
Cal| 494   Fat| 13g   Protein| 8.9g   Carbs| 57.8g   Fiber| 1.5g

Ingredients:

- 240 millilitres (1 cup) whole milk
- 25 grams (2 tablespoons) white sugar
- 30 millilitres (2 tablespoons) rum and coffee liqueur
- 5 millilitres (1 teaspoon) vanilla extract
- 15 grams (1 tablespoon) whipped cream
- 45 grams (3 tablespoons) canned pumpkin
- 120 millilitres (½ cup) hot strong coffee
- 30 millilitres (2 tablespoons) dark rum
- 1¼ grams (¼ teaspoon) pumpkin pie spice plus more for sprinkling

Directions:

1. In saucepan, add milk, pumpkin and sugar over medium heat and cook for about 3-4 minutes or until hot, stirring continuously.
2. Remove the pan of milk mixture from heat and stir in the coffee, liqueur, rum, vanilla extract and pumpkin pie spice.
3. Transfer the latte into large mug and top with the topping of whipped cream.
4. Sprinkle with extra pumpkin pie spice and serve immediately.

Spiked Caramel Latte

Servings|4   Time|10 minutes
Nutritional Content (per serving):
Cal| 307   Fat| 12g   Protein| 6.5g   Carbs| 27.5g   Fiber| 0g

Ingredients:

- ❖ 1 (370-millilitre) (12½-ounce) can hot evaporated milk
- ❖ 80 grams (½ cup) butterscotch chips
- ❖ Pinch of ground cinnamon
- ❖ 360 millilitres (1½ cups) hot coffee
- ❖ 120 millilitres (4 fluid ounces) rum
- ❖ 60 grams (¼ cup) whipped cream

Directions:

1. In a pitcher, add evaporated milk and coffee and stir to combine.
2. Add in butterscotch chips and stir until melted and smooth.
3. Add in rum and stir to combine.
4. Pour into serving cups and top with whipped cream.
5. Sprinkle with cinnamon and serve immediately.

Spiked Macha

Serving|1   Time|10 minutes

Nutritional Content (per serving):
Cal| 268   Fat| 3.8g   Protein| 6g   Carbs| 20.9g   Fiber| 0g

Ingredients:

- ❖ 5 grams (1 teaspoon) matcha powder
- ❖ 180 millilitres (¾ cup) hot whole milk
- ❖ 30 millilitres (2 tablespoons) rum
- ❖ 60 millilitres (¼ cup) hot water
- ❖ 15 grams (½ ounce) simple syrup
- ❖ 30 millilitres (2 tablespoons) Rhum

Directions:

1. Through a tea strainer, sift the matcha powder into a serving mug.
2. Slowly add in (¼ cup) of boiling water, beating continuously.
3. Add the warm milk, simple syrup, rum, and Rhum and beat until well blended.
4. Serve hot.

Jamaica Coffee Cocktail

Serving|1 Time|10 minutes
Nutritional Content (per serving):
Cal| 208   Fat| 49.4g   Protein| 1g   Carbs| 10.8g   Fiber| 0g

Ingredients:

- ❖ 45 millilitres (1½ tablespoons) coffee-flavored liqueur
- ❖ 30 grams (2 tablespoons) whipped cream
- ❖ 45 millilitres (1½ tablespoons) dark rum
- ❖ 240 millilitres (1 cup) hot brewed coffee

Directions:

1. Pour the coffee liqueur and rum into a coffee glass.
2. Fill glass with hot coffee and serve with the topping of whipped cream.

Mulled Cider

Servings|8   Time|1 hour 20 minutes
Nutritional Content (per serving):
Cal| 162   Fat| 0.5g   Protein| 0.5g   Carbs| 36.3g   Fiber| 1.3g

Ingredients:

- 1 whole nutmeg
- 10 whole cloves
- 4 cinnamon sticks
- 1 small orange, cut into slices
- 60 millilitres (¼ cup) rum
- 10 allspice berries
- 2 star anise pods
- 2160-2400 millilitres (9-10 cups apple cider)

Directions:

1. Heat a large-sized, dry saucepan over medium heat and toast the whole spices for about 2-3 minutes, stirring occasionally.
2. Now adjust the heat to low.
3. In the saucepan, add in the apple cider and orange slices and bring to a low simmer.
4. Simmer for about 1 hour.
5. Divide the rum into serving mugs evenly.
6. Through a fine mesh strainer, strain the cider into mugs and serve.

Mulled Orange Wine

Servings|6 Time|3¼ hours
Nutritional Content (per serving):
Cal| 143 Fat| 0.1g Protein| 2.4g Carbs| 11.8g Fiber| 0.4g

Ingredients:

- 1 (750-millilitre) (25-fluid ounce) bottle dry red wine
- 1 orange, sliced into rounds
- 8 whole cloves
- 2 cinnamon sticks
- 60 millilitres (¼ cup) brandy
- 25-50 grams (2-4 tablespoons) white sugar
- 2 star anise pods

Directions:

1. Add wine, brandy, orange slices, sugar, and spices into a large-sized saucepan and stir to combine.
2. Place the saucepan of wine mixture over medium-high heat and bring to a gentle simmer.
3. Now adjust the heat to low and simmer, covered for up to 3 hours.
4. Through a fine mesh strainer, strain the wine mixture.
5. Serve hot.

Mulled Pomegranate Wine

Servings|8   Time|30 minutes
Nutritional Content (per serving):
Cal| 384   Fat| 0.1g   Protein| 0.7g   Carbs| 61.8g   Fiber| 1.3g

Ingredients:

- 2 (750-millilitre) (25-fluid ounce) bottles red wine
- 400 grams (2 cups) white sugar
- 4 lemons, sliced
- 4 cinnamon sticks
- 300 millilitres (1¼ cups) water
- 240 millilitres (1 cup) pomegranate liqueur
- 2 oranges, sliced
- 2½ grams (½ teaspoon) ground nutmeg
- 12 whole cloves

Directions:

1. In a large-sized saucepan, add all the ingredients over medium-low heat and simmer for about 15-20 minutes.
2. Remove from the heat and strain into serving mugs.
3. Serve immediately.

Cranberry Wine Cocktail

Servings|4 Time|20 minutes
Nutritional Content (per serving):
Cal| 291   Fat| 0g   Protein| 0.1g   Carbs| 42g   Fiber| 0.8g

Ingredients:

- ❖ 360 millilitres (1½ cups) cranberry juice cocktail
- ❖ 100 grams (½ cup) white sugar
- ❖ 720 millilitres (3 cups) dry red wine
- ❖ 2 cinnamon sticks
- ❖ 2 star anise pods
- ❖ 50 grams (½ cup) fresh cranberries

Directions:

1. In a saucepan, Add cranberry juice cocktail, cinnamon sticks, star anise and sugar and cook for about 12-15 minutes, stirring occasionally.
2. Add in wine and cranberries and cook for about 4-5 minutes, stirring occasionally.
3. Serve hot.

Buttered Rum

Serving|1   Time|10 minutes
Nutritional Content (per serving):
Cal| 258   Fat| 11.4g   Protein| 0.2g   Carbs| 6.2g   Fiber| 0.1g

Ingredients:

- 10 grams (2 teaspoons) packed brown sugar
- 1¼ millilitres (¼ teaspoon) pure vanilla extract
- Pinch of ground allspice
- 120 millilitres (½ cup) hot water
- 15 grams (1 tablespoon) unsalted butter, softened
- Pinch of ground cinnamon
- Pinch of ground nutmeg
- 60 millilitres (¼ cup) dark rum
- 1 cinnamon stick

Directions:

1. Place the sugar, butter, vanilla extract, and spices into the bottom of an Irish coffee glass or mug and mix well
2. Pour in the rum and top with hot water.
3. Stir well and serve with the garnishing of cinnamon stick.

Lemony Whiskey

Serving|1   Time|10 minutes
Nutritional Content (per serving):
Cal| 151   Fat| 0.1g   Protein| 0.1g   Carbs| 11.8g   Fiber| 0.1g

Ingredients:

- ❖ 180 millilitres (¾ cup) water
- ❖ 45 millilitres (3 tablespoons) whiskey
- ❖ 15 grams (3 teaspoons) honey
- ❖ 10 millilitres (2 teaspoons) fresh lemon juice

Directions:

1. In a small-sized saucepan, add water and bring to a simmer.
2. Pour the hot water into a serving mug.
3. In the mug, add the whiskey, honey, and lemon juice and stir until honey is dissolved.
4. Serve immediately.

Irish Hot Whiskey

Servings|2   Time|10 minutes
Nutritional Content (per serving):
Cal| 151   Fat| 0g   Protein| 0g   Carbs| 12g   Fiber| 0g

Ingredients:

- 16 whole cloves
- 25 grams (2 tablespoons) white sugar
- 2 (45-millilitre) (1½-fluid ounce) jiggers Irish whiskey
- 2 (2½-centimetre) (¼-inch) thick lemon slices
- 360 millilitres (1½ cups) boiling water

Directions:

1. Press 8 cloves into the peel of each lemon slice all the way around. Set aside.
2. Divide the sugar into 2 wine glasses.
3. Arrange 1 metal spoon into each glass with the curved side facing upwards.
4. Pour the boiling water over the back of the spoon in each glass and stir until sugar is dissolved.
5. Divide the whiskey into each glass.
6. Add the lemon slice into each glass and steep for about 1 minute before serving.

85

Non-Alcoholic Mocktail Recipes

Mint Julep

Servings|8   Time|15 minutes
Nutritional Content (per serving):
Cal| 137   Fat| 0g   Protein| 0.2g   Carbs| 35.1g   Fiber| 0g

Ingredients:

- ❖ 200 grams (1 cup) white sugar
- ❖ 150 grams (6 ounces) lemonade concentrate, thawed
- ❖ 30 millilitres (2 tablespoons) water
- ❖ 720 millilitres (3 cups) club soda
- ❖ 25 grams (3 teaspoons) lime juice concentrate
- ❖ 3 drops mint concentrate

Directions:

1. In a saucepan, add sugar and soda over medium heat and stir until sugar is dissolved.
2. Add the lemonade and lime juice and bring to a boil.
3. Remove from the heat and stir in the mint concentrate and water.
4. Refrigerate to chill for about 30-60 minutes.
5. For each serving, add ¼ of cup mixture and ¾ cup of water and mix well.
6. Serve immediately.

Mint Berry Julep

Serving|1   Time|15 minutes
Nutritional Content (per serving):
Cal| 196   Fat| 0.2g   Protein| 1.2g   Carbs| 51.9g   Fiber| 2.3g

Ingredients:

- ❖ 150 millilitres (5 fluid ounces) water
- ❖ 45 grams (1½ ounces) raspberry syrup
- ❖ 15 millilitres (½ fluid ounce) fresh lime juice
- ❖ 1 green tea bag
- ❖ 30 grams (1 ounce) blackberry puree
- ❖ 15 grams (½ ounce) mint infused simple syrup

Directions:

1. In a pan, add water and bring to a boil.
2. Remove from the heat and set aside to cool for about 1 minute.
3. Transfer the water into a container with tea bag and steep, covered for about 2-3 minutes.
4. Remove the tea bag and refrigerate the tea to chill completely.
5. In a cocktail shaker, add tea and remaining ingredients.
6. Cover the cocktail shaker with lid and shake vigorously for about 30 seconds.
7. Strain into a serving glass over ice and serve.

Mango Mojito

Servings|4   Time|15 minutes
Nutritional Content (per serving):
Cal| 142   Fat| 0.4g   Protein| 1.6g   Carbs| 34.6g   Fiber| 2.8g

Ingredients:

- ❖ 30 grams (1 cup) fresh mint
- ❖ 240 millilitres (1 cup) mango juice
- ❖ 15 millilitres (1 tablespoon) fresh lime juice
- ❖ Ice cubes, as required
- ❖ 1 orange, sliced

- ❖ 50 grams (¼ cup) white sugar
- ❖ 240 millilitres (1 cup) orange juice
- ❖ 160 millilitres (2 fluid ounces) seltzer water

Directions:

1. In a pitcher, place the mint leaves and with a muddler, muddle it slightly.
2. Add the sugar and with the muddler, to crush it well.
3. Add in the juices and seltzer water and stir to combine.
4. Fill the serving glasses with ice and top each with mojito.
5. Garnish with orange slices and serve immediately.

Strawberry Agua Fresca

Servings|4   Time|15 minutes
Nutritional Content (per serving):
Cal| 153   Fat| 0.5g   Protein| 1.2g   Carbs| 39g   Fiber| 3.6g

Ingredients:

- ❖ 625 grams (5 cups) fresh strawberries, hulled
- ❖ 90 millilitres (1/3 cup) fresh lime juice
- ❖ Ice cubes, as required
- ❖ 720 millilitres (3 cups) water
- ❖ 100 grams (½ cup) white sugar
- ❖ 1¼ grams (¼ teaspoon) coarse sea salt

Directions:

1. In a high-power blender, add the strawberries and water and pulse until smooth.
2. Though a fine-mesh sieve, strain the puree, pressing with a silicone spatula.
3. Discard the strawberry seeds.
4. Transfer the strawberry puree into a pitcher.
5. Add the sugar, lime juice and salt and stir to combine.
6. Add the remaining enough water to reach the desired consistency.
7. Fill 4 serving glasses with ice cubes and top with strawberry mixture.
8. Serve immediately.

Hibiscus Cocktail

Serving|1   Time|10 minutes
Nutritional Content (per serving):
Cal| 339   Fat| 19.3g   Protein| 3.1g   Carbs| 42.3g   Fiber| 0.8g

Ingredients:

- 90 millilitres (3 fluid ounces) orange juice
- 30 millilitres (1 fluid ounce) fresh lime juice
- 30 grams (1 ounce) cream of coconut
- Ice cubes, as required
- 90 millilitres (3 fluid ounces) pineapple juice
- 15 millilitres (½ fluid ounce) hibiscus grenadine
- 30 millilitres (1 fluid ounce) ginger ale

Directions:

1. In a pitcher, add all ingredients except for ice and mix well.
2. Fill a serving glass with ice cubes and top with juice mixture.
3. Serve immediately.

91

Pina Colada

Servings|2   Time|10 minutes
Nutritional Content (per serving):
Cal| 335   Fat| 21.7g   Protein| 3.1g   Carbs| 37.7g   Fiber| 3.9g

Ingredients:

- 255 grams (1½ cups) unsweetened frozen pineapple chunks
- 10-30 grams (1-3 tablespoons) brown sugar
- 2 fresh pineapple wedges
- 180 millilitres (¾ cup) unsweetened coconut milk
- 180 millilitres (¾ cup) unsweetened pineapple juice
- 4-6 ice cubes
- 2 maraschino cherries

Directions:

1. In a high-power blender, add frozen pineapple chunks, coconut milk, pineapple juice, brown sugar and ice cubes and pulse until smooth.
2. Pour into serving glasses and serve with the garnishing of with fresh pineapple wedges and maraschino cherries.

Citrus Punch

Servings|2   Time|10 minutes
Nutritional Content (per serving):
Cal| 293   Fat| 3g   Protein| 1.7g   Carbs| 66.2g   Fiber| 2g

Ingredients:

- ❖ 310 grams (2 cups) orange sherbet
- ❖ 180 millilitres (¾ cup) water
- ❖ 240 millilitres (1 cup) sprite
- ❖ 20 grams (2 tablespoons) lemonade concentrate

Directions:

1. In a pitcher, add all ingredients and stir to combine.
2. Refrigerate to chill before serving.

Fruity Ginger Ale Punch

Servings|6   Time|10 minutes
Nutritional Content (per serving):
Cal| 170   Fat| 0.2g   Protein| 1g   Carbs| 41.5g   Fiber| 0.6g

Ingredients:

- 960 millilitres (4 cups) mango nectar
- 480 millilitres (2 cups) pineapple juice
- 960 millilitres (4 cups) ginger ale
- 480 millilitres (2 cups) orange juice
- 30 millilitres (2 tablespoons) fresh lime juice
- Ice cubes, as required

Directions:

1. In a pitcher, add all ingredients and stir to combine.
2. Serve immediately.

Colored Punch

Servings|4   Time|15 minutes
Nutritional Content (per serving):
Cal| 290   Fat| 0g   Protein| 0g   Carbs| 75.3g   Fiber| 0g

Ingredients:

For Blue Slush:

- ❖ 480 millilitres (2 cups) sprite soda
- ❖ 100 grams (½ cup) white sugar
- ❖ 2½ grams (½ teaspoon) blue raspberry lemonade kool-aid drink mix
- ❖ 645 grams (3 cups) ice cubes
- ❖ 4 drops neon blue food coloring

For Red Slush:

- ❖ 480 millilitres (2 cups) sprite soda
- ❖ 100 grams (½ cup) white sugar
- ❖ 2½ grams (½ teaspoon) cherry kool-aid drink mix
- ❖ 645 grams (3 cups) ice cubes
- ❖ 4 drops red food coloring

Directions:

1. For blue slush: in a high-power blender, add all ingredients and pulse until smooth.
2. For red slush: in a high-power blender, add all ingredients and pulse until smooth.
3. In 4 serving glasses, place blue slush about ¼ of the way.
4. Now add red slush about ¼ of the way.
5. Repeat until glasses are full.
6. Serve immediately.

Pineapple Coconut Punch

Serving|1   Time|10 minutes
Nutritional Content (per serving):
Cal| 140   Fat| 2.2g   Protein| 0.1g   Carbs| 31.8g   Fiber| 0.7g

Ingredients:

- ❖ 30 millilitres (1 fluid ounce) fresh pineapple juice
- ❖ 90 millilitres (3 fluid ounces) pineapple coconut
- ❖ 60 millilitres (2 fluid ounces) coconut lime sparkling soda
- ❖ Ice cubes, as required

Directions:

1. In a cocktail shaker, place all ingredients.
2. Cover the cocktail shaker with lid and shake vigorously for about 30 seconds.
3. Pour into decorated glass and serve.

Juice Mocktail

Servings|2 Time|10 minutes
Nutritional Content (per serving):
Cal| 227   Fat| 1.9g   Protein| 5.6g   Carbs| 25.3g   Fiber| 17g

Ingredients:

- ❖ 240 millilitres (1 cup) fresh orange juice
- ❖ 240 millilitres (1 cup) guava nectar
- ❖ 240 millilitres (1 cup) passion fruit juice

Directions:

1. In a pitcher, add all ingredients and stir to combine.
2. Serve immediately.

Ginger Ale Mocktail

Serving|3   Time|10 minutes
Nutritional Content (per serving):
Cal| 166   Fat| 0.1g   Protein| 0.4g   Carbs| 42.2g   Fiber| 0.2g

Ingredients:

- ❖ 1440 millilitres (3 cups) ginger ale
- ❖ 480 millilitres (16 fluid ounces) fruit punch
- ❖ 690 millilitres (23 fluid ounces) pineapple juice
- ❖ Ice cubes, as required

Directions:

1. In a pitcher, add all ingredients and stir to combine.
2. Serve immediately.

Fruity Mocktail

Servings|4   Time|10 minutes
Nutritional Content (per serving):
Cal| 621   Fat| 11.8g   Protein| 2.4g   Carbs| 133.3g   Fiber| 0.7g

Ingredients:

- 240 grams (1 cup) heavy whipping cream
- 60 millilitres (¼ cup) passionfruit nectar
- 160 millilitres (2 fluid ounces) cold water
- 55 grams (3 tablespoons) toasted marshmallow syrup
- 60 millilitres (¼ cup) mango nectar
- 35 grams (3 tablespoons) white sugar
- 2 (340-gram) (12-ounce) cans frozen apple juice concentrate

Directions:

1. In a bowl, add the whipping cream, mango nectar, and passionfruit nectar and mix well.
2. Add the sugar and with a hand blender, beat until stiff peaks form.
3. Refrigerate to chill completely.
4. In a high-power blender, add the remaining ingredients and pulse until a slushy texture is achieved.
5. Transfer the mixture into glasses and top with the chilled cream mixture.
6. Serve immediately.

Blue Milk

Servings|2   Time|15 minutes
Nutritional Content (per serving):
Cal| 323   Fat| 15.4g   Protein| 3.2g   Carbs| 47.4g   Fiber| 7.7g

Ingredients:

- 240 millilitres (1 cup) pineapple juice
- 120 millilitres (½ cup) full-fat coconut milk
- 15 millilitres (1 tablespoon) fresh lime juice
- 2 drops blue food coloring
- 120 millilitres (½ cup) rice milk
- 120 millilitres (½ cup) fruit juice
- 15 grams (1 tablespoon) watermelon syrup

Directions:

1. In a high-power blender, add all ingredients and pulse until smooth.
2. Transfer into an ice cream machine and process for about 5-8 minutes or until slushy.
3. Transfer into serving glasses and serve immediately.

Mocktail Brew

Servings|4   Time|15 minutes
Nutritional Content (per serving):
Cal| 414   Fat| 22.5g   Protein| 1.6g   Carbs| 5.5g   Fiber| 0.2g

Ingredients:

For Whipped Cream:

- ❖ 480 grams (2 cups) heavy whipping cream
- ❖ 120 millilitres (½ cup) mango juice
- ❖ 60 millilitres (¼ cup) passionfruit juice
- ❖ 75 grams (6 tablespoons) white sugar

For Brew:

- ❖ 2 (360-millilitre) (12-fluid ounce) cans frozen apple juice
- ❖ (1 cup) cold water
- ❖ 240 millilitres (¼ cup) mango juice
- ❖ 30 millilitres (2 tablespoons) maraschino cherry juice
- ❖ 145 grams (½ cup) toasted marshmallow syrup
- ❖ 430 grams (2 cups) ice cubes

Directions:

1. For whipped cream: in a bowl, add all ingredients and with a hand mixer, mix until a whip cream texture form.
2. Refrigerate to chill before serving.
3. For brew: in a high-power blender, add all ingredients and pulse until smooth.
4. Transfer the mixture into glasses and top with the chilled whipped cream.
5. Serve immediately.

Hot Non-Alcoholic Mocktail Recipes

Hot Chocolate

Servings|4   Time|20 minutes
Nutritional Content (per serving):
Cal| 400   Fat| 23.9g   Protein| 8.7g   Carbs| 46.8g   Fiber| 3.7g

Ingredients:

- 180 millilitres (¾ cup) water
- 720 millilitres (3 cups) whole milk
- 35 grams (3 tablespoons) white sugar
- 60 grams (¼ cup) whipped cream
- 45 grams (3 tablespoons) cocoa powder
- 150 grams (6 ounces) semisweet chocolate, chopped finely

Directions:

1. Place water into a medium saucepan over medium-high heat and bring to a boil.
2. Add in cocoa powder and stir vigorously until smooth.
3. Add in milk and again bring to a boil, stirring continuously.
4. Add in chocolate and sugar and cook for about 5 minutes, whisking frequently.
5. Pour the hot chocolate into four serving mugs and serve with the topping of whipped cream.

Raspberry Hot Chocolate

Servings|4 Time|20 minutes

Nutritional Content (per serving):

Cal| 365   Fat| 19.9g   Protein| 9.1g   Carbs| 38.6g   Fiber| 4.2g

Ingredients:

- ❖ 200 grams (7 ounces) fresh raspberries
- ❖ 15 millilitres (1 tablespoon) water
- ❖ 2½ millilitres (½ teaspoon) vanilla extract
- ❖ 60 grams (¼ cup) whipped cream
- ❖ 25 grams (3 tablespoons) icing sugar
- ❖ 115 grams (4 ounces) dark chocolate, chopped finely
- ❖ 720 millilitres (3 cups) hot whole milk

Directions:

1. Place the raspberries, icing sugar, and water in a small-sized saucepan over medium heat and cook for about 5 minutes, stirring frequently.
2. Through a sieve, strain the raspberry mixture by pressing with the back of a spoon.
3. Discard the seeds
4. Add in the hot milk, chocolate, and vanilla extract in a high-power blender and let it sit for about 1 minute.
5. Add the cooked raspberries and pulse until frothy.
6. Pour the chocolate mixture into mugs and serve with the topping of whipped cream.

Vanilla Steamer

Servings|2   Time|15 minutes
Nutritional Content (per serving):
Cal| 261   Fat| 10.9g   Protein| 10.3g   Carbs| 29.4g   Fiber| 0g

Ingredients:

- 600 millilitres (2½ cups) whole milk
- 1 cinnamon stick
- 30 grams (2 tablespoons) whipped cream
- 40 grams (2 tablespoons) maple syrup
- 10 millilitres (2 teaspoons) vanilla extract
- Pinch of ground nutmeg

Directions:

1. In a saucepan, add the milk, maple syrup and cinnamon over medium heat and cook for about 3-5 minutes, stirring frequently.
2. Remove the pan of milk from heat and stir in the vanilla extract.
3. Pour the milk into a large-sized heatproof container, leaving space from the top.
4. With a milk frother, create the foam in milk.
5. Divide the milk into 2 serving mugs and top each with whipped cream.
6. Sprinkle with nutmeg and serve immediately.

Orange Mocha

Servings|6   Time|20 minutes
Nutritional Content (per serving):
Cal| 104   Fat| 2.3g   Protein| 3.5g   Carbs| 19.8g   Fiber| 1.5g

Ingredients:

- ❖ 3-4 orange peel strips
- ❖ 2 cinnamon sticks
- ❖ 480 millilitres (2 cups) water
- ❖ 90 millilitres 1/3 cup fresh orange juice
- ❖ 60 grams (¼ cup) unsweetened cocoa powder
- ❖ 1¼ millilitres (¼ teaspoon) vanilla extract

- ❖ 7 whole cloves
- ❖ 480 millilitres (2 cups) whole milk
- ❖ 85 grams (½ cup) brown sugar
- ❖ 390 grams (2 tablespoons) instant coffee crystals

Directions:

1. In a spice bag, wrap the orange peel strips, cinnamon, and cloves.
2. In a large-sized saucepan, add in the spice bag and remaining ingredients except for vanilla extract over medium heat and cook until boiling, stirring continuously.
3. Remove the saucepan of mixture from heat and set aside, covered for about 10 minutes.
4. Discard the spice bag and stir in vanilla extract.
5. Serve hot.

Gingerbread Latte

Servings|2   Time|10 minutes
Nutritional Content (per serving):
Cal| 215   Fat| 8.5g   Protein| 6.6g   Carbs| 30g   Fiber| 0.7g

Ingredients:

- 180 millilitres (¾ cup) strong-brewed coffee
- 10 grams (2 teaspoons) white sugar
- 5 grams (1 teaspoon) ground ginger
- 30 grams (2 tablespoons) whipped cream
- 35 grams (2 tablespoons) molasses
- 5 grams (1 teaspoon) ground cinnamon
- 360 millilitres (1½ cups) hot whole milk

Directions:

1. In a glass bowl, combine the coffee, molasses, sugar, and spices and beat until well blended.
2. Divide the coffee mixture into two mugs.
3. Top with milk and serve with the topping of whipped cream.

Spiced Cider

Servings|4   Time|45 minutes
Nutritional Content (per serving):
Cal| 124   Fat| 0.3g   Protein| 0.3g   Carbs| 31.3g   Fiber| 1.2g

Ingredients:

- ❖ 960 millilitres (4 cups) apple cider
- ❖ 45 millilitres (3 tablespoons) clementine juice

- ❖ 12 star anise pods
- ❖ 1 cinnamon stick
- ❖ 3 whole cloves
- ❖ 3 whole allspices berries

Directions:

1. In a medium-sized saucepan, add all ingredients over medium heat and bring to a boil.
2. Now adjust the heat to low and simmer for about 30 minutes.
3. Strain the spices and serve hot.

Cranberry Cider

Serving|12   Time|1 hour
Nutritional Content (per serving):
Cal| 166   Fat| 0.4g   Protein| 0.6g   Carbs| 40.9g   Fiber| 1.4g

Ingredients:

- ❖ 1920 millilitres (8 cups) soft apple cider
- ❖ 2 medium oranges, sliced
- ❖ 50 grams (¼ cup) white sugar
- ❖ 3 cinnamon sticks, broken into pieces
- ❖ 11920 millilitres (8 cups) unsweetened cranberry juice
- ❖ 1 (5-inch) (2-inch) piece fresh ginger, peeled
- ❖ 8-10 whole cloves
- ❖ 3 star anise pods
- ❖ 2 cardamom pods

Directions:

1. Add in apple cider and cranberry juice into a large-sized saucepan over medium-high heat and bring to a boil.
2. Add in orange slices, ginger, sugar and spices and stir to combine
3. Now adjust the heat to low and simmer for about 45 minutes.
4. Strain the mixture and serve hot.

Pear Cider

Servings|2   Time|15 minutes
Nutritional Content (per serving):
Cal| 621   Fat| 1.5g   Protein| 4g   Carbs| 164.6g   Fiber| 36g

Ingredients:

- ❖ 10-12 pears under-ripe, halved and cored
- ❖ 1-2 cinnamon sticks
- ❖ 8-12 allspice berries
- ❖ 4-6 whole cloves
- ❖ 1 star anise pod

Directions:

1. Add all pears into a juicer and extract the juice according to the manufacturer's method.
2. Through a large-sized cheesecloth, strain the juice.
3. In a spice sachet, place the whole spices.
4. In a large-sized saucepan, add about 720-840 millilitres (3-3½ cups) of strained pear juice with spice sachet over medium-high heat and bring to a boil, stirring occasionally.
5. Remove the pan of juice from heat and set aside, covered for about 5-10 minutes.
6. With the back of a spoon, press the spice bag to release any excess liquid.
7. Then discard the spice bag.
8. Transfer the cider into serving mugs and serve.

Cranberry Mocktail

Serving|1   Time|15 minutes
Nutritional Content (per serving):
Cal| 159   Fat| 0.3g   Protein| 0.8g   Carbs| 31.4g   Fiber| 6.6g

Ingredients:

- ❖ 180 millilitres (¾ cup) cranberry juice
- ❖ 1 (1¼-centimetre) (½-inch) piece fresh ginger, peeled
- ❖ 5 grams (1 teaspoon) honey
- ❖ 90 millilitres (1/3 cup) orange juice
- ❖ ½ cinnamon stick
- ❖ 2 whole cloves

Directions:

1. Place the cranberry juice, orange juice, ginger, and spices into a small-sized saucepan over medium heat and bring to a gentle simmer.
2. Now adjust the heat to low and simmer for about 2 minutes.
3. Remove the pan of Mocktail from heat and stir in the honey.
4. Strain into a serving mug and serve.

Buttered Pineapple Mocktail

Servings|6   Time|35 minutes
Nutritional Content (per serving):
Cal| 170   Fat| 4.2g   Protein| 1.1g   Carbs| 33g   Fiber| 0.5g

Ingredients:

- ❖ 1440 millilitres (6 cups) pineapple juice
- ❖ 30 grams (2 tablespoons) butter
- ❖ 4 cinnamon sticks, broken
- ❖ 150 millilitres (10 tablespoons) orange juice
- ❖ 10 grams (2 teaspoons) brown sugar

Directions:

1. Add in the pineapple juice, orange juice, butter, brown sugar, and cinnamon sticks into a large-sized saucepan and bring to a boil.
2. Now adjust the heat to low and simmer for about 20 minutes.
3. Strain into serving mugs and serve.

Hot Wassail

Serving|10   Time|1 hour 5 minutes
Nutritional Content (per serving):
Cal| 149   Fat| 0.8g   Protein| 0.7g   Carbs| 36.4g   Fiber| 1.9g

Ingredients:

- 2 apples
- (8 cups) apple cider
- 90 millilitres (1/3 cup) lemon juice
- 4 cinnamon sticks
- 1¼ grams (¼ teaspoon) ground nutmeg
- 15 whole cloves
- 1920 millilitres (2 cups) orange juice
- 10 grams (1 tablespoon) light brown sugar
- 1¼ grams (¼ teaspoon) ground ginger

Directions:

1. Poke the cloves into the skin of apples on all sides.
2. Place the apples and remaining ingredients over medium-high heat and bring to a boil.
3. Now adjust the heat to medium-low and simmer for about 30-45 minutes.
4. Remove from the heat and discard the apples and whole cloves.
5. Transfer into mugs and serve.

Orange Atole

Servings|4   Time|25 minutes
Nutritional Content (per serving):
Cal| 222   Fat| 3.1g   Protein| 5.2g   Carbs| 45.8g   Fiber| 0.9g

Ingredients:

- ❖ 360 millilitres (1½ cups) water
- ❖ 240 millilitres (1 cup) orange juice, strained
- ❖ 480 millilitres (2 cups) hot whole milk
- ❖ 40 grams (6 tablespoons) cornflour, sifted
- ❖ 100 grams (½ cup) white sugar

Directions:

1. Blend the water and cornflour in a saucepan until the flour dissolves completely.
2. Place the saucepan over high heat and cook for about 3-5 minutes or until the mixture is thick, stirring continuously.
3. Add the orange juice and sugar and cook for about 2-3 minutes, stirring continuously.
4. Add the milk and stir to combine well.
5. Cook for about 5 minutes, stirring continuously.
6. Serve hot.

Hot Toddy Mocktail

Serving|1   Time|10 minutes
Nutritional Content (per serving):
Cal| 73   Fat| 0.4g   Protein| 0.2g   Carbs| 18.9g   Fiber| 0.7g

Ingredients:

- ❖ 5 millilitres (1 teaspoon) lemon juice
- ❖ 1¼ grams (¼ teaspoon) ground cloves
- ❖ 150 millilitres (5 fluid ounces) hot tea
- ❖ 1 lemon wedge
- ❖ 20 grams (1 tablespoon) honey
- ❖ 1¼ grams (¼ teaspoon) ground cinnamon
- ❖ 1¼ grams (¼ teaspoon) ground nutmeg

Directions:

1. In a serving mug, add lemon juice, honey and spices and stir until well combined.
2. Pour the hot tea into the mug and stir to combine well.
3. Garnish with the lemon wedge and serve immediately.

Citrus Cranberry Tea

Serving|6   Time|35 minutes
Nutritional Content (per serving):
Cal| 47   Fat| 0g   Protein| 0.1g   Carbs| 10.2g   Fiber| 1.4g

Ingredients:

- 200 grams (2 cups) fresh cranberries
- 1 cinnamon stick
- 60 millilitres ¼ cup) fresh orange juice
- 40 grams (2 tablespoons) honey
- 1440 millilitres (6 cups) water
- 4 whole cloves
- 15 millilitres (1 tablespoon) fresh lemon juice

Directions:

1. In a large-sized saucepan, add cranberries, water, cinnamon sticks and cloves over high heat and bring to a boil.
2. Reduce the heat to low and simmer, covered for about 15-20 minutes.
3. Remove the pan of tea from heat and through a cheesecloth lined colander, strain the tea.
4. Return the tea into the same pan and stir in the remaining ingredients.
5. Place the pan of tea over medium-low heat and simmer for about 4-5 minutes or until heated completely.
6. Serve hot.

Citrus Green Tea

Serving|1   Time|10 minutes
Nutritional Content (per serving):
Cal| 52   Fat| 0.2g   Protein| 0.5g   Carbs| 12.5g   Fiber| 0.2g

Ingredients:

- ❖ 1 (5-centimetre) (2-inch) lemon zest piece
- ❖ 10 grams (2 teaspoons) green tea powder
- ❖ 120 millilitres (½ cup) grapefruit juice
- ❖ 10 grams (2 teaspoons) honey
- ❖ 10 millilitres (2 teaspoons) boiling water
- ❖ 180 millilitres (¾ cup) hot water
- ❖ 25 millilitres (5 teaspoons) lemon juice

Directions:

1. In a large-sized mug, add lemon peel and 10 millilitres (2 teaspoons) of boiling water and brew, covered for about 3 minutes.
2. Add green tea powder and hot water and stir to combine.
3. Now, add the grapefruit juice, lemon juice and honey and stir until well combined.
4. Serve hot.

Printed in Great Britain
by Amazon

87278509R00068